JUNKANOO
COSTUME CONSTRUCTION
(A BEGINNER'S GUIDE TO JUNKANOO DESIGN)

DR. EMMANUEL W. FRANCIS
(JUNKANOO LEGEND)

PREFACE

This book is an attempt to assist teachers and group leaders in their efforts to educate students and group members about the basics of junkanoo costume construction and design.

This has become necessary to ensure that the skills we have learned are passed on to our successors in a more formal way; especially as junkanoo is introduced into the school curriculum in the Bahamas.

Moreover, too many junkanoo participants are ignorant of the basic fundamentals of costume construction and are totally dependent upon designers to do all the work. This often leads to mass production and ill-fitting costumes that participants are helpless to correct.

TABLE OF CONTENTS

INTRODUCTION

I was formally introduced to junkanoo costume construction by my brother, Percy (Vola), and the Saxons in the fall of 1966 at the age of fifteen while attending G.H.S.

In those days, junkanoo costumes were basically fringed pants, shirts, boots and hat or national dress e.g. Romans, Beefeaters, which copied those designs. Sometimes designers became more creative and portrayed birds, insects, flowers, deck of cards, etc. but pants and shirts remained the main covering.

Cardboard was the material of choice for flat designs but chicken wire and tie wire were used to achieve three dimensional designs. This made it necessary to cover the wire for fringing by sewing cloth to it. Cardboard was also sewed together with mason line and sail needle.

We observed that the pants and shirts became ragged and unsightly particularly in the seat, arm pits and neck after only a short period of parading. This occurred because the fringed crepe paper began to fall off when the home-made flour pap glue we used dissolved from wetting by perspiration.

Boxing Day, 1969, I introduced the four piece costume design concept to cover up this flaw and give the Saxons a competitive edge. This ensured clean neat costumes at the end of the parade, and is the standard of costume construction today.

In this exercise, my goal is to focus on the basics of costume fabrication in the hope that participants in Jr. and Sr. parades will be better equipped to take a more proactive role in the making of their own costumes.

CHAPTER 1

MATERIALS, SUPPLIES AND SAFETY

Cardboard (clean)
Tie wire (10 gauge)
Contact cement
Masking tape (1")
White semi-gloss paint
Lead pencil (#2)
Ball point pen
Permanent marker (black)
Meter ruler (preferably metal)
Paint brushes (2")
Latex or rubber gloves
Felt cloth (1 yd.)
Foam rubber (1/4" – 1/2" thick)
Metal shears or box cutter
Cutting pliers (6" – 9")
Staple machine (optional)
Work bench
Refuse bin
Adequate ventilation
First aid kit
Safety goggles

SANITATION:

- Working area should be clean and uncluttered.
- Materials used must be clean and sanitary.
- All refuse should be immediately placed in refuse bins.
- Eating and drinking not permitted in work area.
- Hands should be washed before and after eating.
- Hands and tools (e.g. brushes) should not be placed in the mouth.
- Spitting, urinating, etc. should not be allowed in work area.
- Persons with active respiratory infections (e.g. influenza) should not enter the work area, unless outdoors.
- Pets are not permitted in work area.

SAFETY:

- Work area is not the place for playing and fooling around with tools, materials and supplies.
- Safety goggles should be worn at all times to avoid eye injuries.
- Work area must have adequate ventilation, especially when contact cement is to be used. Vapors from contact cement are

harmful and the lid should be allowed to close after each dip with the contact brush, and sealed tightly after use.

- Contact cement vapors are flammable and should never be used near an open flame, or where sparks may occur.
- Smoking is prohibited in the work area because of the danger from igniting contact cement fumes and also the health risks to others from second hand smoke.
- Rubber or latex gloves are recommended when using contact cement or paint to avoid the absorption of harmful chemicals through the skin.
- Contact cement will bond most surfaces together but they must be clean and dry. Simply apply a single coat of contact liquid to both surfaces, allow to dry (about fifteen minutes), press surfaces firmly together; this creates a strong, permanent bond.
- Extreme care must be taken when using box cutters and even shears to avoid injury. Always remember to keep body parts out of the path of the cutting instrument when using them.
- First aid kit should be readily available as injuries can happen, especially to children. It is not advisable to put these dangerous tools and materials in the hands of young children.

- Clean hands and sanitary working conditions reduce the risk of infection should physical injury occur. An adequate supply of water is necessary to flush the eyes and skin should they be contaminated with chemicals.
- All work should be done on a work bench to ensure proper posture while working and avoid stress on the muscles, joints and spine.
- Working on the floor or ground should be prohibited also because it is unsanitary.
- Contamination of the work area with body fluids, e.g. saliva, urine, etc. can create health risks as well and should be vehemently discouraged.

CHAPTER 2

BASICS OF COSTUME DESIGN

(The Four Piece Concept)

The four piece costume concept was designed to ensure the neatness of the costume even after profuse sweating and rigorous parading. This became necessary to cover the scrappy looking pants and shirt that lost their fringe as we rushed throughout the morning hours.

The four pieces are: hat, shoulder piece, back piece and front piece; the latter three to cover the pants and shirt.

The back piece is what we call "the skirt" today.

The shoulder piece was designed to cover the shoulders, drape around the neck and cover the chest and back as well. This allowed for intricate designs to be placed in this area without fear of being ruined by the effects of hours of rushing and sweating.

Over the years, the shoulder piece has become so elaborate that it has created its own individual category as "Off the Shoulder" dancers, which is beyond the scope of this book.

The back piece was designed to hide the ragged looking pants around the waist, hips and the back and sides of the thighs. Like the shoulder piece, this too created an area for application of durable designs, enhancing the beauty of the back of the costume.

Back pieces have also evolved to elaborate "skirts" with imaginative trappings and appendages as junkanoo artisans displayed their collective, creative geniuses in costume designing.

The front piece was added to cover the front of the pants which included the fly and the front of the thighs. It was also necessary to hide the hook which fastened the back piece in the area of the belt buckle.

Needless to say, this front piece also created an area for various design patterns to be incorporated into the overall design of the costume.

The four piece design was responsible for much of the success of the Saxons in the 1970's, and other groups later adopted this style of costuming, which is the standard of junkanoo design today.

CHAPTER 3

CROWN CONSTRUCTION

The crown is defined as the part of the hat that fits snugly on the head like the crown of a king, and is the foundation on which the hat is built.

An ill-fitting crown is a junkanoo's worst nightmare and often presents when hats are mass produced for a generic, hypothetical head size, to be adjusted later. It is annoying to see participants holding their hats on their heads while trying to rush. Every junkanoo must see to the proper fabrication of his/her crown before their hat is built.

The crown should be custom made to comfortably fit the owner without falling off while parading. A properly fitted crown is not too tight, and does not need elastic bands to stay in place.

PRACTICAL

Materials and supplies needed:

Cardboard

Felt

Contact cement

¼" or ½" foam rubber sheet 6" x 24"

Metal shears or box cutter

Meter ruler

Permanent marker

Paint brush (2")

(A) OLD FASHIONED CROWN

Step 1:   Cut a rectangular piece of card-board 6" x 30".

Step 2:   Cut a rectangular piece of felt to cover the cardboard piece with enough to lap over one edge 7" X 30".

Step 3:   Wet one surface of the cardboard with contact and apply the felt to it while wet. Leave 1" of felt to lap over the edge.

Step 4:   Turn the cardboard over and brush contact on the 1" felt flap and along the adjacent cardboard edge (1" wide) and allow to dry (about 10 -15 minutes).

Step 5: Press the felt flat to the cardboard firmly to complete the lapping process.

Step 6: Cut a piece of ½" foam (6" x 24"), wet inner surface of cardboard with contact and press foam to it while wet. Allow to dry (5 – 10 minutes).

Step 7: Wrap the foam part around the head, adjust to a tight, comfortable fit and mark with marker.
(N. B. The foam size will probably be too big, cut away the excess foam to match the head size. This will avoid overlap of the foam. Measure and mark again).

Step 8: Apply contact cement to opposing surfaces within the mark and allow it to dry.

Step 9: Stick only a small portion together and recheck the fit. When the fit is confirmed, press parts together firmly.

The cylinder is now complete.

Step 10: Place the cylinder on the head with the lapped surface at the bottom, mark the location of the ears and cut out a semi-circular slot for them. Mark the front on the inside of the cylinder, this is important.

Step 11:   Place the cylinder on the head, set the front to eye brow level, mark location of the top of the head and cut away that excess at the top.

Step 12:   Stand the top of the cylinder on a piece of cardboard and mark the circle. Draw another circle around that one with a 1" longer radius. Cut out the larger circle and clip the edge to the inner circle. This will be used for the top of the crown.

Step 13:   Wet the top outer 1" of the cylinder and the clipped edge of the circle with a layer of contact cement and allow it to dry.

Step 14:   Press contacted surfaces together firmly.

CROWN IS NOW COMPLETE.

(Celebrate by beating on it like a drum).

OLD FASHIONED CROWN

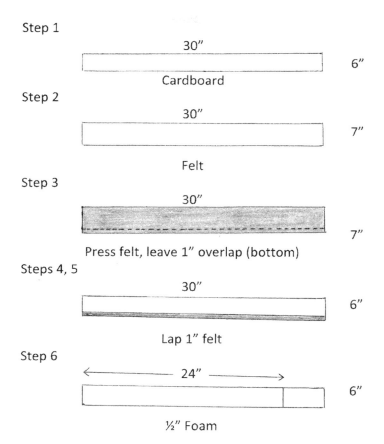

Step 1

30"

6"

Cardboard

Step 2

30"

7"

Felt

Step 3

30"

7"

Press felt, leave 1" overlap (bottom)

Steps 4, 5

30"

6"

Lap 1" felt

Step 6

24"

6"

½" Foam

Step 7, 8

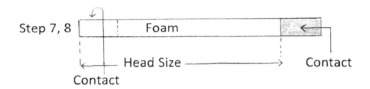

Foam

Contact — Head Size ——→ Contact

Contact

Step 9

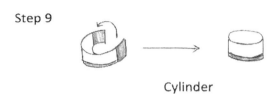

Cylinder

Step 10   (Slot for ears)

Mark Front ——→

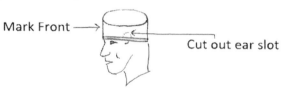

Cut out ear slot

Step 11

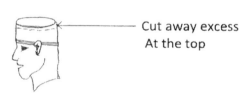

Cut away excess
At the top

Crown Construction

Circle for top of cylinder

Step 12

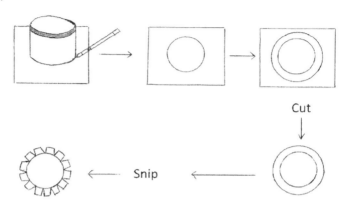

Cut

Snip

Step 13, 14

Apply Contact and bond

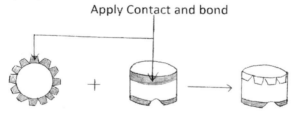

(B) MODERN OR TAPERED CROWN

Materials and Supplies:
Cardboard
Felt fabric
Contact cement
½" foam rubber
Paint brush (2")
Meter ruler
Permanent marker
Metal shears or box cutter
6" - 8" Cutting pliers
10 gauge Tie wire
Industrial size stapler (optional)

Step 1: Cut a rectangular piece of card-board 3" x 30" parallel to the grains of the cardboard. Similarly, cut 2 rectangular pieces of cardboard 3" x 15".

Step 2: Mark and fold the cardboard pieces lengthwise to create double thickness.

Step 3: Cut 3 pieces of tie wire to lengths of the cardboard and straighten them manually.

Step 4: Push the wire through one of the grains of the cardboard away from the edge along the full length of it. Cut away any excess wire. (The wire acts like a skeleton, stiffens the cardboard and allows it to be bent into different shapes).

Step 5: Brush contact on the folded surfaces of the cardboards and allow it to dry.

Step 6: Press fold together to create double thickness for the three strips.

Step 7: Cut three pieces of felt 4" wide to cover both surfaces of the cardboard strips.

Step 8: Brush one surface of each cardboard with contact cement and apply felt leaving ½" over the edge while the contact is still wet.

Step 9: Brush the other side of the strips and lap the remaining felt while contact is wet. Allow them to dry (10 minutes).

Step 10: Cut away the excess felt and reglue any weak felting areas.

Step 11: (optional): Take the long strip and apply ¼' foam rubber to one surface about 24".

Step 12: Bend this strip into a circle, wrap around the head and mark head size.

Step 13: Cut off excess strip leaving about 2" for bonding.

Step 14: Re-measure fit and bond with contact cement or adequately staple in place to create a head band.

(If stapling, make sure raw edges of staple is on the outside, away from the head).

Step 15: Attach one of the other strips on the outside of the ban at the back, place the band on the head down to the ears, bring the strip over the top of the head and mark at the front to fit.

Step 16: Cut the strip to the mark and attach to the band. (Mark the front).

Step 17: Attach the other strip to the band across the top of the head just in front of the ears. Cut away any excess strip. (N.B. Bend the sharp edges of the wire in the strips away from the edge and parallel to the head band).

MODERN CROWN IS NOW COMPLETE:

Enjoy the moment!

QUESTIONS COMMONLY ASKED ARE:

1. Why do we recommend felting of the cardboard?

Cardboard can fall apart when wet with sweat. Bonding felt to it with contact cement ensures that this will not happen.

2. Why is it necessary to line the crown with foam rubber?

Foam rubber lining is not essential but allows for a tighter fitting crown that is more comfortable.

3. Which of the two crowns is better?

The old fashioned crown is bigger and provides more support for larger hats.

The modern crown is smaller and shaped more like the human head. This allows for smaller hat size and is ideal for hat designs that taper to the head.

MODERN CROWN

Step 1   Cut cardboard strips

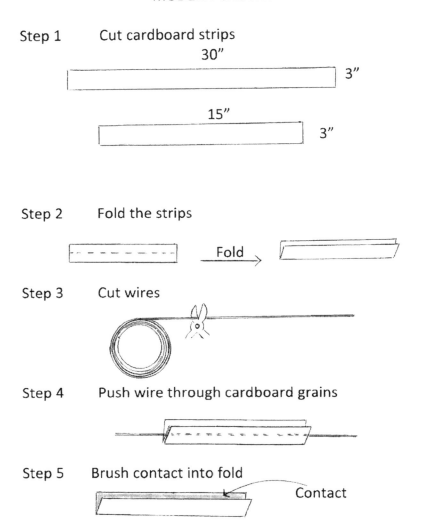

30"

3"

15"

3"

Step 2   Fold the strips

Fold

Step 3   Cut wires

Step 4   Push wire through cardboard grains

Step 5   Brush contact into fold

Contact

Step 6   Press fold together

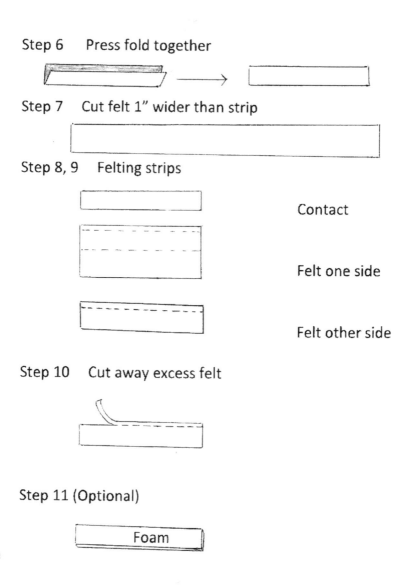

Step 7   Cut felt 1" wider than strip

Step 8, 9   Felting strips

Contact

Felt one side

Felt other side

Step 10   Cut away excess felt

Step 11 (Optional)

Foam

Step 12, 13   Bend long strip into circle for head sizing.
              Cut head band for 2" overlap.

Step 14   Bond with contact cement.

Step 15, 16   Attach front to back strip.

Step 17   Attach side to side strip.

Finished crown

CHAPTER 4

HAT CONSTRUCTION

Materials and supplies:

Crown
Cardboard
Contact cement
10 gauge Tie wire
Permanent marker
Metal shears or box cutter
Hat design

Basics of hat construction:

The hat can be basically divided into four parts. These are crown, center piece, front piece and back piece.

Center Piece:

This is the tallest part of the hat and is drawn to design, cut out and strengthened with wire before being attached across the middle of the crown from right to left. The center piece provides the outline of the frontal view of the hat and is the first piece attached to the crown.

N. B. It is important that the center piece be designed with the grains of the cardboard in the vertical plane, allowing for easy folding of the cardboard at the mid-line and assures symmetry between right and left sides.

The design should be no larger than about 16" tall x 14" wide.

Center piece design:

Step 1:   Using the meter ruler, draw a horizontal line 14" long for the base and
a vertical line 16" at the mid-line
for the height. Fold the cardboard
along the vertical line and, with a
pencil, draw the design using the
mid-line for reference. This would
usually be a rough sketch.
Once the design is satisfactory, outline the left side of the design with
the permanent marker and cut out
neatly.
Fold the cardboard and mark the
right side with a ball point pen or
pencil to match the left side.
Cut out right side.

N. B. Some hat designs are built around a profile or side view which requires a center piece connected to the middle of the crown from front to back. These pieces are obviously not symmetrical.

Step 2:   A slot is cut at the bottom of the center piece at the mid-line to fit the full size of the crown. Care must be taken when cutting to leave flap extensions at the top and sides for crown attachment. These flaps are pre-folded to fit the crown.

Step 3:   The center piece is then strengthened with wire strips that run horizontally and vertically. The vertical wires can easily be pushed through the grains of the cardboard but horizontal ones usually need to be fastened on top of the cardboard with contact cement and thin ¾" strips of cardboard.
It is important for the wires to extend the full length of the cardboard including the flaps.
The vertical wire at the mid-line could extend about 6" beyond the top of the center piece and be bent into a hook for easy handling or hanging.

Step 4:   Bend the flaps toward the front at a right angle. Place the crown in the slot with the centre piece just in front of the ears. Be sure the center piece is aligned properly and mark with a permanent marker to ensure accurate bonding.

Step 5: Brush contact cement to underside of the flaps and areas marked on the crown for bonding. Allow to dry, (about 10 minutes) and fasten center piece to the crown.

Front Piece Design

Step 6: The purpose of the front piece is to hide the crown, (especially the old fashioned one) and give dimension and design to the front of the hat. The height should be just above the top of the crown and extend in width to reach the center piece on both sides.

Step 7: The front piece should be symmetrical, like the center piece, and strengthened similarly with vertical and horizontal wires after design and cutting.
Before bonding, bend the front piece to adapt to the front of the crown at the bottom.

N. B. Only the bottom of the front piece is attached to the crown. This allows for the top to be flared outward   creating additional dimension to the crown.

Mark clearly to ensure flared position on bonding.

Step 8:   Attach the front piece to the crown with contact cement at the midline first and move outward. Do not press firmly until flared position is confirmed.

Back piece design

Step 9:   The purpose of the back piece is to hide the back of the crown and give structural support to it.
Cut a piece of cardboard 12" high with vertical grains and extend in width to meet the center piece on each side.

Step 10:   Temper the cardboard by temporarily rolling it into a tight cylinder which allows for ease in molding it to the desired shape.

Step 11:   Cut the top 3" in the shape of an arch without reducing the height and make a 4" slice down the middle to a height just above the crown.

Step 12: Pull both sides of the slice toward the mid-line so that they overlap creating the shape of a ½ dome at the top.

Step 13: Place against the hat to ensure a closed fit and mark overlap for bonding. Bond overlap with contact cement or staple.

Step 14: Fit the back piece to the hat and mark for bonding. Bond back piece to crown and center piece while keeping the ½ dome shape intact.

HAT IS NOW COMPLETE:
(Celebrate!) .... NOW!

HAT CONSTRUCTION

Step 1   Center piece

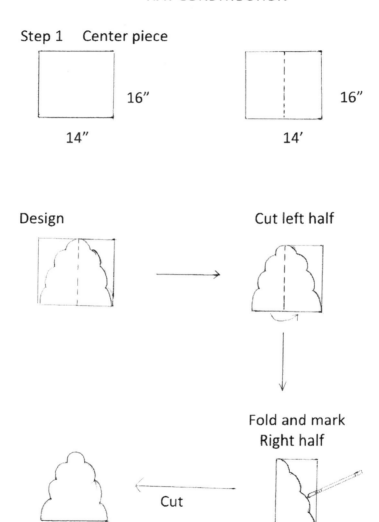

16"

14"

16"

14'

Design

Cut left half

Fold and mark
Right half

Cut

Step 2

Mark slot for crown

Draw and cut flaps

Crown

Fold flaps

Step 3

Hook

Vertical wires

BACK

Horizontal wires

¾" Cardboard strips

Hat Construction

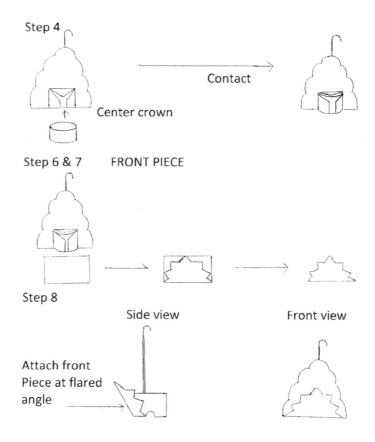

Step 4

Contact

Center crown

Step 6 & 7   FRONT PIECE

Step 8

Side view   Front view

Attach front
Piece at flared
angle

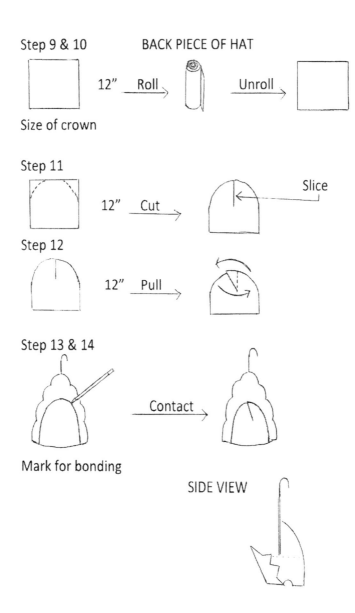

Step 9 & 10

BACK PIECE OF HAT

12" Roll → Unroll →

Size of crown

Step 11

12" Cut →

Slice

Step 12

12" Pull →

Step 13 & 14

Contact →

Mark for bonding

SIDE VIEW

CHAPTER 5

SHOULDER PIECE CONSTRUCTION

Materials and supplies:

Cardboard

Contact cement

Felt

10 gauge Tie wire

Metal shears or box cutter

Cutting pliers

Permanent marker

Meter ruler

Masking tape

2 pencil

Step 1:   Draw a cardboard circle of about 28" in diameter using a radius made from tie wire. To do this, cut a 16" piece of wire and bend both ends 1" from the edge into a right angle. Tape the tip of the pencil to one end and punch the other end through the cardboard for the center of the circle. This creates a home-made mathematical divider.

Hold the wire at the center with one hand and use the pencil attachment to mark the circumference of the circle with the other hand.

N. B. The simplest shoulder piece is just a circle. This circle size is designed for adult males whose shoulders are usually much broader than females and children.

The size of the circle should be customized to fit the person using it.

Step 2:   Temporarily roll the circle into a tight cylinder along the grains of the cardboard to ensure smooth adaptation to the shoulders. The grains will run horizontally.

Step 3:   Cut out a small circle at the center with a diameter slightly larger than the width of the neck and strengthen this area with a felt circle to about 4" on the under-side.

Remember to lap the felt at least 1" on to the top surface. Felt protects against tearing at the neck.

Step 4:   Cut 1" slices around the circle about 1" apart. This creates flexible flaps for the head to pass through without widening around the neck.

Step 5:   Cut two pieces of wire about 24"
           and contact to the underside of
           the circle across the grains using 1"
           cardboard strips placed about 3"
           from the neck area.
Step 6:   Similarly bond two shorter pieces
           of wire, about 18", to the underside
           about 3" from the outer edge.
Step 7:   Bend the circle to arch over the
           shoulders, chest and back.

BASIC SHOULDER PIECE IS NOW COMPLETE:

(When a fringed shirt is not required)

N. B. Boxing in the sides of the shoulder
piece is necessary to cover fringe defects at
the shoulders and arms when fringed shirts are
required.
Step 8:   To box in the shoulder piece cut
           two pieces of cardboard 8" wide
           x 10" tall with the grains running
           horizontally.
Step 9:   Trim the top into an arch I" larger
           than the curvature of the shoulder
           piece at the shoulder.
Step 10:   Snip 1" flaps on the sides and arch
           of the side pieces and bend for

attachment to the shoulder piece. Flaps in the area of the arch could be trimmed on the sides to avoid overlapping when bonded.

Step 11: Bond flaps to the shoulder piece with contact cement.

SHOULDER PIECE IS NOW COMPLETE:
(Enjoy the moment!)

NOTES:

1. Shoulder pieces can be made from fabric instead of cardboard for a softer fit.

2. Side pieces can be replaced by side flaps to increase range of motion; e.g., brass musicians who would be hindered from playing by side pieces.

SHOULDER PIECE

Step 1

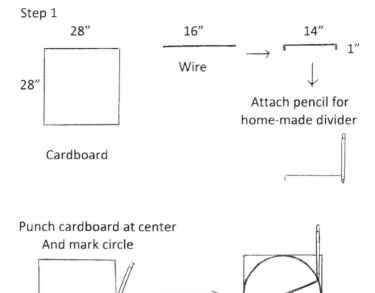

28"

28"

Cardboard

16"

Wire

14"

1"

Attach pencil for
home-made divider

Punch cardboard at center
And mark circle

Cut

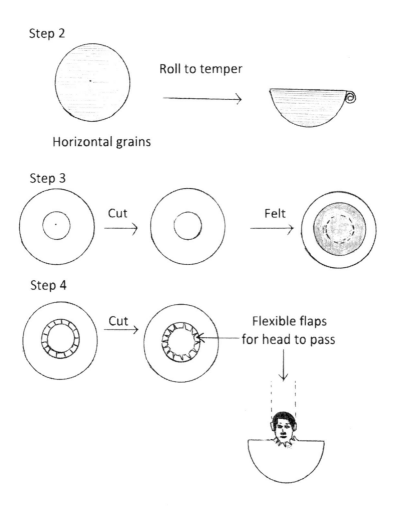

Step 2

Roll to temper

Horizontal grains

Step 3

Cut

Felt

Step 4

Cut

Flexible flaps
for head to pass

Step 5

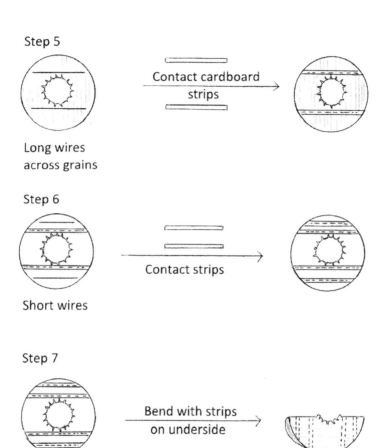

Contact cardboard
strips

Long wires
across grains

Step 6

Contact strips

Short wires

Step 7

Bend with strips
on underside

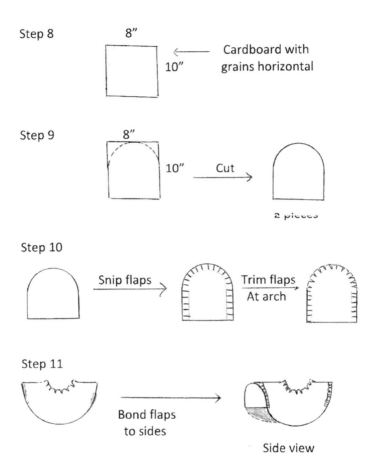

Step 8

8"

10"

← Cardboard with grains horizontal

Step 9

8"

10"

Cut →

2 pieces

Step 10

Snip flaps →

Trim flaps
At arch →

Step 11

Bond flaps
to sides →

Side view

CHAPTER 6

WAIST BAND CONSTRUCTION

Materials and Supplies:

Cardboard

Contact cement

Felt

10 gauge Tie wire

Wire cutter

Metal shears or box cutter

Meter ruler

Marker

Step 1:   Cut a rectangular piece of cardboard 4" wide x waist size length and fold lengthwise down the middle.

Step 2:   Cut a piece of tie wire 2 x waist + 15" to stiffen waist band and make a wire hook for the skirt.

Step 3:   Bend the wire in half creating a 1and1/2" wide loop in the middle.

Step 4:   Brush contact cement on the folded surface of the band.

Position the wire down the middle with each strip 1" apart, and fix the loop to extend 1" beyond the cardboard. The other ends of the wire will extend beyond the cardboard and serve as hooks for the waist band when they pass through the loop on closure.

Step 5:   Press the folds firmly in place to ensure bonding. To avoid injury, bend the raw ends of the wires into a small, tight loop.

Step 6:   Cover the waist band with felt using contact cement.

WAIST BAND IS NOW COMPLETE:

N. B. The waist band is the most important part of the back piece or skirt.

Like the crown, it must be custom made, sturdy and comfortable.

Waist Band Construction

Step 1

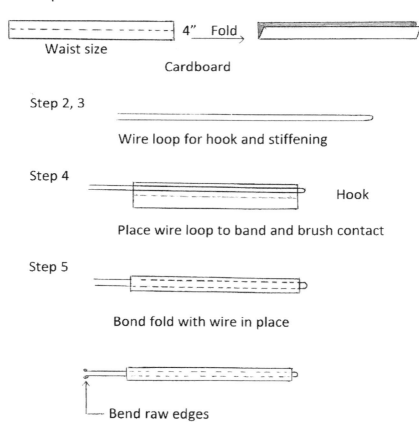

4"   Fold

Waist size

Cardboard

Step 2, 3

Wire loop for hook and stiffening

Step 4

Hook

Place wire loop to band and brush contact

Step 5

Bond fold with wire in place

Bend raw edges

Step 6

Cover both sides of band with felt

Finished waist band

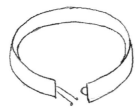 

CHAPTER 7

SKIRT BACK PIECE CONSTRUCTION

Materials and Supplies:

Cardboard

Contact cement

Felt

10 gauge Tie wire

Wire cutter

Metal shears or box cutter

Marker

Meter rule

Step 1: Cut a piece of cardboard about 20" high and waist size wide with the grains vertical.

Step 2: Temporarily roll the cardboard into a tight cylinder to ensure smooth curvature of the back piece around the hips.

Step 3: Draw the bottom 1/3 of the cardboard into an arch, using the midline to assure symmetry, and cut out.

Step 4: Strengthen the cardboard with two horizontal wires 5" from the top and bottom using 1" cardboard strips and contact cement.

Step 5:   Bend the cardboard to curve around the waist and hips and pre-pare for attachment to the waist band.

Step 6:   Cut 2" slices about 2" apart at the top of the cardboard and bend outward to create flaps for attachment.

Step 7:   Attach to the waist band with con-tact cement ensuring that the card-board flares outward at the bottom.

Step 8:   Secure the attachment area with a felt flap along the entire length using contact cement.

BACK PIECE IS NOW COMPLETE:

N. B.   The flaring of the back piece must NOT be so high that it exposes the hips. This happens often, even with experienced designers, and defeats the main purpose, which is to cover this area.

BACK PIECE CONSTRUCTION

Step 1

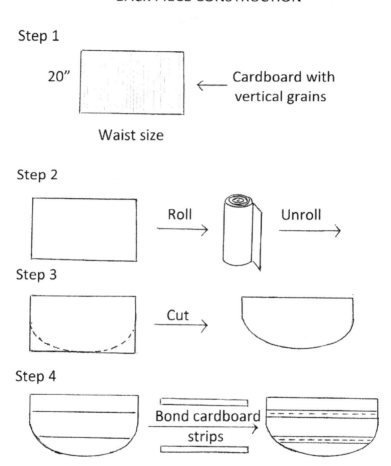

20" — Cardboard with vertical grains

Waist size

Step 2

Roll → Unroll →

Step 3

Cut →

Step 4

Bond cardboard strips →

Horizontal wires

Step 5

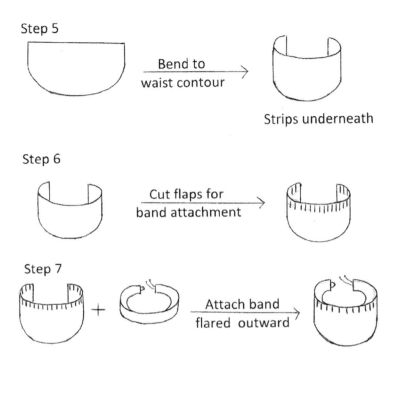

Step 6

Step 7

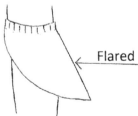

Step 8

Contact felt $\longrightarrow$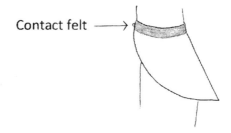

CHAPTER 8

FRONT PIECE CONSTRUCTION

Materials and Supplies:

Cardboard
Contact cement
10 gauge Tie wire
Wire cutters
Metal shears or box cutter
Meter ruler
Marker

Step 1:   Design a piece of cardboard about 18" tall and 7" wide at the top with the grains vertical. The width at the bottom should not exceed the width of the body.

Step 2:   Reinforce the cardboard by con-tacting two horizontal wires with 1" cardboard strips.

Step 3:   Create a hook for the front piece using tie wire.

Cut a piece of wire about 40" long and bend into a 1" wide loop at the middle.

Step 4:   Bend the other ends of the wire 2"
            from the end to form right angles
            from right to left.
Step 5:   Center the wire on the underside
            of the cardboard so that the loop
            extends about 7" above the top
            and mark.
Step 6:   Contact the wire to place using 6' X
            12" cardboard strap.
Step 7:   Bend the loop downward to create
            a 7" long hook on the underside of
            the front piece.

FRONT PIECE IS NOW COMPLETE:

N. B. The back piece is put on first and hooked
at the front using the wire hooks.

The front piece goes on after and loops
behind the back piece hook at the center.

FRONT PIECE CONSTRUCTION

Step 1

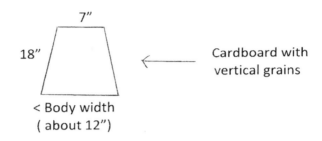

7"

18"

< Body width
(about 12")

Cardboard with
vertical grains

Step 2

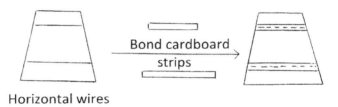

Horizontal wires

Bond cardboard
strips

Step 3

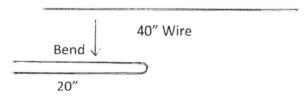

40" Wire

Bend ↓

20"

Step 4

Step 5

Step 6

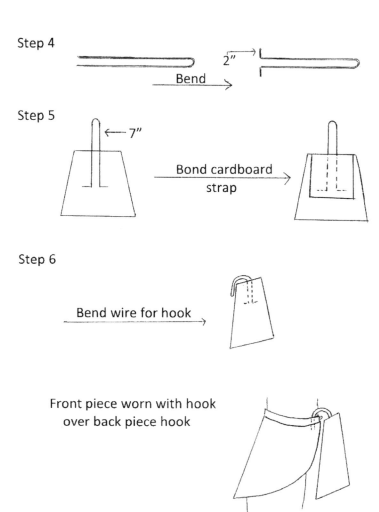

Bend

2"

7"

Bond cardboard strap

Bend wire for hook

Front piece worn with hook over back piece hook

CONCLUSION

I have attempted to present a systematic step by step guide to the basics of costume design and construction based on more than forty years of experience in this area.

It is important to follow the exact sequence to achieve the best results. The hat is made first because it is the most important part of the costume and is the key to the design of the other pieces.

A section on safety is critical to this exercise as far too many participants are susceptible to injury or infection when using junkanoo materials and supplies for the first time. Time must be spent to ensure that they learn the fundamental risks involved before working on their costumes.

Costumes should never be considered more important than people, and every effort must be made to ensure their comfort and safety. Unfortunately, the intensity of the junkanoo competition often puts winning as the number one priority at the expense of personal safety.

God has given us creative genius which allows us to make these magnificent costumes and we should never worship them as our gods. When we keep junkanoo in its proper place, we will be better able to enjoy it. Remember, God first, people second, costumes last.

Enjoy the experience, live well and love life.